I0173517

Snichimal Vayuchil

Translated by
Paul M. Worley

North Dakota Quarterly

NDQ

Supplement

This work is licensed under the Creative Commons Attribution 4.0 International License. To view a copy of this license, visit http://creative-commons.org/licenses/by/4.0/ or send a letter to Creative Commons, PO Box 1866, Mountain View, CA 94042, USA.

ISBN-13: 978-0692073612 (Digital Press at The University of North Dakota, The)
ISBN-10: 0692073612

2018
North Dakota Quarterly
in collaboration with
The Digital Press at the University of North Dakota.

For more on *North Dakota Quarterly*, go here: ndquarterly.org

For more on The Digital Press at the University of North Dakota, go here: thedigitalpress.org

Snichimal Vayuchil

Snichimal Vayuchil
EXPERIMENTAL POETRY IN BATS'I K'OP

Paul M. Worley

Snichimal Vayuchil or Flowery Dream is an experimental poetry workshop in bats'i k'op, or Tsotsil Maya, where writers create poetry in their own mother language and Spanish, sharing their work as a form of what they call relational poetry. The workshop is also a place where these young writers reflect upon the origins of literature in indigenous communities, as well as the contributions contemporary indigenous literary creation makes to social change.

As a collective, here individual workshop members present two of their poems in English translation with the goal of reaching as wide an audience as possible. You'll find a good deal of sonic diversity, Tsostil and its twin, Spanish (translated here into English of course!), and in some cases multiple languages are used for poetic composition. This bilingualism underscores the writers' abilities and knowledge across languages. Composing in free verse, the poets express their daily lives, painting landscapes from the urban and rural imaginaries, to share their thoughts about land, family, love, pain, death, la lucha, resistance, and many other things to give a voice to those usually denied a voice, music to the deaf, in poetic composition! We hope you enjoy.

Experimento poético en Bats'i K'op

Snichimal Vayuchil o Sueño Florido es un taller experimental de poesía en bats'i k'op, lengua tsotsil, donde los escritores producen poesía en su propia lengua y en español, y que además se comparten en un espacio llamado poesía relacional. El taller Snichimal Vayuchil también es un espacio donde las personas pueden reflexionar sobre los orígenes de la literatura en los pueblos indígenas, así como de las creaciones contemporáneas de los pueblos indígenas y sus aportes a los procesos de cambio social.

En este trabajo encontraremos una diversidad sonora, que mezclándose entre la lengua tsotsil, y su par, el castellano, se juegan ambas para componer algunos versos, que muestra la habilidad al autor en el manejo y conocimiento de cada lengua. Entre las formas de escribir, que son de formato libre, los autores expresan y comparten su cotidianeidad, pintando cada paisaje en el imaginario comunitario o citadino, sus sentires con la tierra, la familia, el amor, el dolor, las muertes, la lucha, la resistencia, y muchos otros elementos que buscan dar voz a los sin voz, y ¡a los sordos, poesía!

Así, los compañeros del taller, ahora colectivo, presentan dos de sus creaciones para ser traducidas al inglés con la idea de ser publicados en una página en internet.

Bilanguaging the Political Literary Landscape of Maya Tsotsil Autonomous Poetic Projects

Gloria E. Chacón

Abya-Yala, the land of maturity in the Guna language, or the continent baptized as Latin America in the nineteenth century, has been gradually experiencing a significant literary and artistic transformation since the late 1970s.[1] The conforming aesthetic terms, imported and imposed on indigenous nations, are altered and contested through the multi-lingual literary projects that are becoming central to intellectual debates in the study of contemporary literature. This epistemic undoing gains strength through the work of various social actors, with writers representing a central element in these changes. Poetry, as the most popular form of expression stands at the helm of this contemporary literary revolution. Historically, indigenous poetry has been intimately associated with song, prayer, and various religious rituals and spiritual pursuits. Plato dismissed poetry as a vain and corruptive activity that is removed from truth and reason. In contrast, Mesoamerican communities--according to the preserved historical records —venerated their poets who descended from the erudite and priestly class. Pictures of speech scrolls or <u>volutes</u> in Mesoamerican histories, whether these stood for song, chants, history, myth, or musical instruments, illustrate some of these literary practices in Pre-Columbian texts and other cultural

[1] Albó, Xavier. "Our Identity Starting From Pluralism in the Base." In *The Postmodernism Debate in Latin America*, edited by John Beverley, José Oviedo and Michael Aronna, 18-33. Durham: Duke University Press, 1995.

artifacts. In addition to the political novelty and promise that the Zapatista movement came to signify around the world, Chiapas also represents the epicenter and site/sight of Maya literary production with the formation of various entities focused on its creation and dissemination since the 1980s.

Indigenous literatures from Abya-Yala share similar, fundamental themes and issues with Native American Literature, however, key divergences also distinguish them from one another. According to the literary critic, Molly McGlennen, Native American Literary nationalism in the twentieth century has focused predominately on narratives and autobiography and less significantly on poetry, a genre deployed mainly by indigenous women in the United States. McGlennen's discussion of Native literature also notes that in the US context, "indigenous women poets highlight some of the limitations of nationalistic approaches to understanding their work just as it suggests how central tribal identity is."[2] In counter distinction, for Latin America, indigenous literary movements and their critics have tended to focus heavily on poetry. McGlennen argues for an in-depth analysis of poetry, because it offers different ways of thinking about indigeneity as it intersects with questions of displacement, diaspora, and queerness.

Another fundamental disjuncture between the Turtle Island and Abya-Yalan literary issues pertains to the subject of translation and its complexities. The vast majority of indigenous poets and writers in Latin America tend to publish bilingually, for two particular reasons. Although, the fundamental principal in writing in an indigenous language is grounded on the necessity of preservation and conservation, it is nonetheless a political act of defiance that is informed by decolonization at

---

[2] McGlennen, Molly. *Creative Alliances. The Transnational Designs of Indigenous Women's Poetry.* Norman: University of Oklahoma Press, 2014, 7.

its core, whereas the Spanish and English language versions allow their literary works wider reach, transcending their local origins. Relatedly—and not unproblematically-- writing in a Maya or Zapotec language has tended to serve as the primary identification of a writer as a indigenous, which is not the case for Native writers in Canada or the United States who tend to publish monlingually. Assuming this double movement between languages is closer to the notion of bilanguaging as Walter Mignolo and Allen Chadwick discuss, signaling that this creative act does not refer explicitly to the act of translating from one language to the other but moving between two or more languages and cultural systems, and actively engaging the politics of their asymmetry. Bilanguaging and translation facilitates the intercultural dialogues poets and other indigenous and non-indigenous politicized agents strive to establish for more equitable social relations. *Snichimal Vayunchil*'s (Flowered Dream) translation into the English language also becomes an important source of support for the ten young and emergent contributors to the anthology. It is precisely this grassroots project, created in poetry workshops, that needs to be heard and disseminated beyond the small number of copies printed. The poetry gathered in this anthology comes from a unique perspective of "relation" where Bats'i k'op (Tsotsil language or 'real' language) and the Spanish languages can convey the import of literature for indigenous peoples as well as a space where the indigenous language is not subordinate to the European one and where indigenous identity is reaffirmed.

Snichimal Vayuchil is a beautiful, cultural artifact that appeals to all the senses. From the illustrated cover that invites the hand to feel its texture to the handwriting announcing its title and the intimate conversation between the contemporary and pre-Columbian image and the text, this anthology represents another important contribution to the renaissance of indigenous literatures in the Americas. The poems brought together treat various themes: death, politics, love, women, solitude, spirituality, geography and cultural elements. The poets do not create in isolation, manifesting concerns with indigenous autonomies and ontologies as in Manu Pukuj's "La prisa" (The Hurry), a poem that emphasizes an alternative stream of time and life. The poem embraces the natural rhythm of life because the speaker is "one with the leaves on the trees/ which die and are reborn in due time." The speaker moves at the rate of a different compass because they (neutral pronoun) are "rooted in the flavors/and pleasures of fruits that comes and goes," alluding to a misguided separation of humanity and nature. Awareness that this sense of fast pace is external to indigenous communities is palpable in the fifth stanza: "That's why: this hurry, it's not my hurry/ the hurry of time,/the hurry of the few,/the hurry of slavery, the hurry of money." Poetry participates in deconstructing a system that values materialism over life. In the last couplet the speaker turns to universal edicts, "Because I've seen that love doesn't hurry, because I've seen that life and death don't hurry." The speaker rejects a mechanical or automated lifestyle and returns to a restored sense of balance where life and death follow their cycles.

In a similar fashion, "Danzar" ("Dance") by Cecilia Díaz presents a speaker who affirms an indigenous ontology by favoring dance as ritual. The speaker describes dancing with dreams, speaking to the sacred fire (story telling), dancing (communicates) with the ancestors, and using incense that saturates her body, making her heart dance (happy). The incense melts fears, the bitterness of the world, fights death and keeps vengeance at bay. Repetition in the first stanza offers readers a particular rhythm that originates in the oral tradition of prayer. Standing alone, the last line presents a quick, linear message, and the punch line of the poem-- that I loosely translate as—"I dance to destroy your clock/ time "Y yo danzo destruyendo tu reloj" implies a rejection to a mechanized, factory configuration of time. These poets offer the reader glimpses into indigenous ontologies, thereby making tangible that other ways of living and relating to the world are possible.

Candelaria Álvarez

O'ot

Vo'nej xa nak'al komel ana'ele
tik'il k'alto ta yutil jvayech
¡Manchuk o'ot no'ox !

Xa jax o ti jvayeche
ak'obe stsak ti jkuxlejale
sk'ak'al avinkilale slajes te sike.

Manchuk o'ot no'ox,
Nak'alot ti yut jvayech.

Tú

Eras un pasado atrapado,
mis sueños más profundos
¡eras sólo tú!

Acariciabas mis sueños,
tus manos tocaban mi alma,
tú calor mataba al frío.

Sólo eras tú,
atrapado entre mis sueños.

You

You were an imprisioned memory,
my wildest dreams,
you and only you!

You caressed my dreams,
your hand touched my spirit,
your warmth dissipated the cold.

But you were only you,
imprisioned in my dreams.

La Voz Del Alma

Corazones que pronuncian tu nombre
almas que se llenan de tristeza
te buscan en los sueños
no pueden ver tu rostro.

Penétrate, deja verte
no te vayas, no te escondas
regresa a los sueños floridos
los sueños que tocan las puertas de la esperanza,
de los corazones despiertos
de las almas que quieren ser escuchadas,
de aquellos sentimientos nobles,
floridos alrededor de la vida.

Spirit Voice

Hearts that pronounced your name,
spirits filled with sadness
seeking you in dreams,
unable to see your face.

Come in, be seen
don't go, don't hide
come back to the flowered land
of dreams opening doors to hope,
of waking hearts
of spirits that want to be heard,
of those noble feelings
flowering around existence.

2

Cecilia Díaz

Uni Ants

Uni ants, uni ants
stsebot jch'ul me'etik U
stsebot jch'ul totik K'ak'al
xanavan, xanavan ta vitsetik
ch'ailteso ta pom.

Xa xchi'inot ti k'analetike,
xa smeyot ti ch'ul ak'obale.

Xa k'opon ti totil me'iletike
xa k'eojinta jch'ul me'tik balumile
xa ak'otaj xchi'uk ch'ul ik'
xa tse'in xchi'uk ajovil ch'ulel.

K'upino akuxlejale, nom xa k'el batel
te xlok' xa tal jtotik k'ak'ale.

Uni ants, uni ants, likan xa me!

Mujercita

Mujercita, mujercita
hija de la madre Luna
hija del padre Sol
camina, camina a las montañas
y dales de tu copal.

Te guían las estrellas
la noche te abraza.

Reza a los abuelos
canta a la sagrada madre tierra
danza con el sagrado viento
ríe con tu enloquecido espíritu.

Ama la vida mujercita y mira al horizonte
que ya viene naciendo el padre Sol.

Mujercita, mujercita: ¡despierta ya!

Little Woman

Little woman, little woman
daughter of the Moon
daughter of the Son
walk, walk in the mountains
and burn your copal* for them.

Guided by stars,
the night embraces you.

Pray to our ancestors,
sing to our sacred Mother Earth,
dance with the sacred wind,
smile with your wild spirit.

Love life, little woman, and look to the horizon,
our Father Sun is already rising.

Little woman, little woman: wake up!

*Copal is an incense commonly used in rituals in the Highlands of Chiapas.

Ak'otajel

Avi chi ak'otaj xchi'uk jvayijel
avi chi ak'otaj xchi'uk ch'ul k'ok'
avi chi ak'otaj xchi'uk me'il totil.

Ti pome sch'ailtes jtakupal
smuyubajes ko'on.

Ti pome ja' slajes jxi'eltik
ta schoplejal balumil
slajes milbail
slajes uts'intael.

Vo'one chi ak'otaj ta sokesel areloj.

Danzar

Hoy danzo con mis sueños
hoy danzo con el fuego sagrado
hoy danzo con mis ancestros.

El copal sahuma mi cuerpo
hace danzar mi corazón.

El copal derrite los miedos
la amargura del mundo
asola la muerte
abate la venganza.

Y yo danzo destruyendo tu reloj.

Dance

Today I dance with my dreams
today I dance with the sacred fire
today I dance with my ancestors.

The copal clothes my body
making my heart dance.

The copal melts my fears
the bitterness of this world
defying death
denying vengeance.

And I dance, unwinding time.

Manu Pukuj

La Prisa

La prisa, no es mi prisa,
porque me junto con las hojas de los árboles
que mueren y retoñan sin prisa.

Porque me fundo en el sabor
y en el placer de las frutas que van y vienen,
de las vueltas y revueltas de mamá tierra y papá sol.

Porque me acoplo en el canto de las aves
y en el soplo del viento sin prisa.

Porque vi que el amor no tiene prisa,
porque vi que el vivir y el morir no tienen prisa.

Por eso: la prisa, no es mi prisa
es la prisa del tiempo
es la prisa de unos cuántos
es la prisa de la esclavitud
es la prisa de la moneda.

¡Oh! Hermanos míos
la prisa que llevo no es mi prisa:
es la prisa del tiempo
es la prisa de unos cuántos
es la prisa de la esclavitud
porque vi que el amor no tiene prisa
porque vi que el vivir y el morir no tienen prisa.

Y tú, ¿tienes prisa?

Hurry

This hurry, it's not my hurry,
because I'm one with the leaves on the trees
who die and are reborn in due time.

Because I'm rooted in the flavors
and pleasures of fruit that comes and goes,
the revolutions and evolutions of Mother Earth and Father
    Sun.

Because I am one with the song of the birds
and breathe the song of the lazy breeze.

Because I've seen that love doesn't hurry,
because I've seen that life and death don't hurry.

That's why: this hurry, it's not my hurry
the hurry of time,
the hurry of the few,
the hurry of slavery,
the hurry of money.

Oh, my brothers,
this hurry I carry isn't mine:
it's the hurry of time,
it's the hurry of a few,
it's he hurry of slavery,
it's the hurry of money.

Because I've seen that love doesn't hurry,
because I've seen that life and death don't hurry.

And you, are you in a hurry?

Vovijel

Oy k'usi k'ux ta ko'on
xk'unim ko'on
chi ok'
li' jch'ulele la svol sba
la sch'ay sba batel
mu xa xka'i bu oy
yu'un li chibesat
la jnuptan vokol ta be
ja' yu'un la jch'ay jba batel ta ko'on.

Xi jk'oplal:

indio mugroso pata rajada.
Salí de aquí.
Pinche indio, no sabes nada.
No seas indio, hablá bien.

Jun k'ak'al
xi, ilo'ilaj ko'on ta kaxlan k'op:

¡Sí, y qué!

Sí, sí acepto que mi pata es rajada
porque aún acaricio la tierra,
nos palpamos, nos conectamos,
nos alimentamos.

Esa mugre que nombras es la tierra
soy de tierra, soy yo mismo.
Es sagrada y por ella soy sagrado.

Sí, sí acepto salir de aquí y de allá
con mi pie descalzo y rajado

porque no tiene límites
porque creo en un mundo sin límites,
ni fronteras en los valles, montañas y mares
para seguir sintiendo el calor y
las caricias de mi Sagrada Madre.

Sí, sí acepto humildemente que aún no sé nada.
Pero, indio en la India. Tsotsil, cultura milenaria maya.
México, división política.

Sí, sí acepto hablar bien para decirte que me siento bien
al haber expresado estas palabras.

Xi, ilo'ilaj ko'on
xi lok' ta alel ku'un.

Vovijel

Oy k'usi k'ux ta ko'on
xk'unim ko'on
chi ok'
li' jch'ulele la svol sba
la sch'ay sba batel
mu xa xka'i bu oy
yu'un li chibesat
la jnuptan vokol ta be
ja' yu'un la jch'ay jba batel ta ko'on.

Xi jk'oplal:

You dirty indian with your bare feet.
Get out of here.
Fucking stupid Indians.
No Tonto talk, speak right.

Jun k'ak'al
xi, ilo'ilaj ko'on ta kaxlan k'op:

Yeah, so what?!

I accept my bare feet
so I can caress the earth,
we touch each other, connected,
we sustain each other.

That filth? That filth is the earth,
I'm from the earth, that's me.
It's sacred, and so I'm sacred.

Yes, I go everywhere
with my bare, calloused feet
because the earth has no limits
because I believe the world is infinite,
without borders in the valleys, mountains, and seas
I'll keep feeling the heart
and the embrace of Mother Earth.

Yes, I'll humbly accept my ignorance.
But Indians are from India. The Tsotsil are a millenarian
    Maya people.
Mexico, a political division.

 Yes, I'll use proper grammar to tell you that saying this feels
    good.

Xi, ilo'ilaj ko'on
xi lok' ta alel ku'un.

YUTSIL O'ONTONAL

Mi cha sa' li k'anele
mu xa sa' li lekil satile
sa'o li o'ontonale
sa'o li kuxlejale.

Ak'o ta ilel slekil ach'ulele
jech k'ucha'al li k'analetike.
Ak'o ta ilel li avo'ontone
ti k'usba cha nope.

Ti o'ontonale sna'
buchu stak' cha chi'in ta xanbal
buchu stak' cha chi'in ta ok'el
li' ta osil banumil.

Li kuxlejale ja' vinajel,
jech k'ucha'al smuil nichimetik
jech k'ucha'al chk'ejin mutetik
svok'ebal k'anbail.

K'ano xchu'uk tuk'ulano li akuxlejale.
Pixo xchu'uk albo ti avo'ontone.

Li o'ontonale te oy ta snopbenal
li chiname te oy ta o'ontonal
cha nop xchu'uk ajol avo'onton
cha k'an batel ap'ijilale.

La Belleza Del Corazón

Si buscas amor
no te aferres a la belleza
busca el corazón
busca la vida.

Enseña la belleza del alma
como las estrellas de mi noche.
Habla con el corazón
como sueños en el horizonte.

El corazón sabe
con quién andar
con quién llorar
en la piel de la tierra.

La vida es un cielo,
es aroma de flores
como el canto de pájaros,
donde brota el amor.

Ama y cobija en nuestra vida.
Abriga y conversa con tu corazón.

El corazón en la cabeza,
el cerebro en el pecho,
pensarás con amor,
amarás con sabiduría.

Beauty Of The Heart

If you are looking for love
don't cling to beauty
look for the heart,
look for life.

Teach the beauty of the soul
like the stars of my night.
Speak from the heart
like dreams on the horizon.

The heart knows
who to walk with
who to cry with
on the face of this earth.

Life is heaven,
the aroma of flowers
like the birds' song
where love grows.

Love and shelter your life,
shelter and speak with your heart.

The heart in your head,
the heart in your chest,
you'll think with love,
you'll love with wisdom.

Vaychil Ta Kuxlejal

Chi kuxi ta jvaych xka'i
mu jk'an xi julav
kuxlejale ta jvayche
ja' lek yutsil ta melel.

Jvaychin yaxal osilaltik
jvaychin asikil avutsilal
ta xkil ti abontake
ta jk'el ti avo'ontone.

Mu jk'an xi julav
lek ti li' oyote
mu jk'an xi ok'
mu jk'an xi julav ta ach'ulel…

Soñar En La Vida

Quiero vivir soñando
no quiero despertar
porque la vida en mis sueños
es más justa que la realidad.

Sueño paisajes verdes
sueño la frescura de tu ser
veo los colores de tu piel
veo tu corazón crecer.

No quiero despertar
quiero estar junto a ti
no quiero llorar
no quiero despertar en tu inocencia…

18

DREAMING IN LIFE

I want to live dreaming
I don't want to wake up
because in my dreams life
is more just than reality.

I dream green landscapes
I dream the newness of your being
I see the colors of your skin
I see your heart swell.

I don't want to wake up
I want to be near you
I don't want to cry
I don't want to awaken in your innocence...

Rola Vago

ACH' SLIKEBAL

Ta yut asat, xmuyubaj avo'onton
xtajin ach'ulel, xjinet avinkilal
yu'un oy ach' slikebal.

La vaychinon, mu xa sibtes avayech
cha vil ta nom, slekil akuxlejal
ta yantik buch'u smak asat.

Mu'yuk k'usi lek bik'it
mu'yuk k'usi lek muk'
li stak' ta tael me xkak' ta ko'ontontik.

Te yach'il slikebal kuxlejalil.

NUEVO COMIENZO

La alegría de tu corazón, expresa tus ojos
tu alma armoniosa, te da fuerza y seguridad
porque hay un nuevo comienzo.

Tus sueños son aves de libertad
anda ve y vuela, no dejes de caminar
no escuches quien desvanece tu sombra.

No hay sueños pequeños
no existen sueños eternos
que no se pueda alcanzar con el corazón.

Nuevamente comenzar en la vida.

New Beginning

Your heart's joy, the expression of your eyes
your balanced soul, give you strength and certainty
because things are beginning again.

Your dreams are free birds,
go, see, and fly, don't stop walking
don't listen to those who diminish your shadow.

There are no small dreams,
there are no eternal dreams,
that can't be achieved in one's heart.

Life begins again.

VAYECH

Vayech ta vinajel
vayech ta banamil
ch'ulelal ta jvinkilal
ch'ulelal ta jlap'.

Ta asat oy jk'elum
ta asat oy jch'iel
ta jlekil, ta jchopolil.

Oyun ta ak'ob
oyun ta avelov
oyot ta jbek'tal
smuk'ul, ch'ul vayechil.

DREAMING

Starry dreams
terrestrial dreams
my spirit in my body
my spirit in my breath.

In your gaze I am a seed
in your gaze I grow
evil or beautiful.

Your arms envelop me,
prostrate before you
because you live in my body
you are hope, the flowered dream.

SUEÑO

Sueños siderales
sueños terrenales
espíritu de mi cuerpo
espíritu de mi aliento.

En tu mirada soy semilla
en tu mirada soy crecimiento
del mal o del bien.

Tus brazos me cobijan
ante ti postrado estoy
porque vives en mi cuerpo
eres esperanza, sueño florido.

23

Ruve K'ulej

JUN AK'OBAL

Jun ak'obal nilik batel, ni xanav ta sjol vitsetik,
laj ka'i k'ux'elan xk'ejin li ja'maletike
xchi'uk li chonbolemetike.

Li ak'ubale laj yip li jbek'tale
laj yik'un ta xanobal ta kuxlejale.

Ja' no'ox li jch'ulele sna' bu ayem ta xanavel,
ta sa'el yipal ta stilet ta yik'al vinajel.

UNA NOCHE

Una noche desperté, recorrí las montañas,
escuché el canto de los bosques
y el aullido de los animales.

La noche absorbió mi cuerpo,
y su aliento guió mis ansias en la vida.

Sólo mi alma recuerda su viaje al infinito
buscando alimentarse del soplo del universo.

One Night

I awoke one night, I ran through the mountains,
I listened to the song of the woods
and the howling animals.

Night absorbed my body,
its breath calming my anxieties.

Only my soul recalls its sojourn to the infinite,
as it nurtured itself in the breath of the universe.

Vaech

Oy kuxlejal ta sjunul balumil
ni jvok'utik
ni jch'ikutik
ni vachajkutik
chi jchamkutik batel ta sjunul osil balumil k'uchel xtiltun
    k'analetike.

Soñar

Hay vida en todo el universo
nacimos
crecimos
soñamos
nos morimos en el universo
como la luz intermitente.

Dream

There is life throughout the universe
we are born
we grow
we dream
we die in the universe
we are intermittent light.

Vu'un

Pomun, ta jmuiltas
o'ontonal ta bitomajel.
Ta jmuyubajes ti buy ts'ijil
jun ch'ulel ta ok'el.

Sikil nichimun, ta sakubel osil
ya'lel sat ti k'un yaman sobe.

Ts'ijil ak'obalun
jik'el o'ontonal yu'un vaychilun.

Vu'un ta jk'upin slekil avuni sat
jlik pok' ta xmuy batel ta vinajel
jech k'ucha'al slametel k'ok' ta smuil pom.

Soy

Soy incienso que perfuma
el latido del corazón.
Soy alegría del alma
que en silencio llora.

Soy la flor fresca de la mañana,
lágrimas de la tibia aurora.

Soy el silencio de la noche
el suspiro del sueño.

Soy quien contempla la esencia de tu ser
el pañuelo que se eleva al cielo
como fuego lento con aroma de copal.

I Am

I am the incense that perfumes
the heartbeat.
I am the soul's happiness
that weeps in silence.

I am the fresh morning flower,
tears of the warm dawn.

I am the nocturnal silence,
the sigh-filled dream.

I am the one who contemplates your being
the scarf rising toward the sky
like a slow fire smelling of copal.

Sk'in Ch'ulelal

Estáticas las cruces
que marcan los cuatro recintos del universo
la guitarra, el sot, al ritmo de la danza.
El copal con la ardiente braza
que diluye el aroma del pom.

Poco a poco las velas se consumen
como la vida que nos disipa
como el aroma de la juncia que se expande
como las flores que envejecen.

Las copas del pox
recorren nuestras venas.
Las jícaras de pajal ul
humedecen nuestros labios.

Con los brazos caídos, abatidos por la música
el aire se filtra, en nuestros rostros pálidos
que secas están, como las tumbas de tierra
poco a poco nos enterramos,
como nuestras emociones sigilosas.

Sk'in Ch'ulelal

The four crosses
that mark the four corners of the universe
are immovable
the guitar, the maracas, the rhythm of the dance.
Copal added to the burning embers
dilutes the sweet-smelling pom.

Little by little the candles devour themselves,
like our disappearing existence
like the expanding scent of the sedge
like aging flowers.

Cups of pox
run through our veins.
Jícaras from the gourd tree
moisten our lips.

Our arms fallen, weakened with music,
the air distills our pallid faces
as dry as earthen graves
for these silent emotions.

Paty López

Sts'ujulil Xk'uxul O'ontonal

Ta yech'omal ave'e
vinik antsetik
la smal sk'uxul yo'ontonik.

Takin nichimal satil
ta sk'elik jch'ul metik banamil
te chalbik ti oy svokolike.

¿K'ucha'al?
¿k'ucha'al ti ta chalbunkutik indioe?

Manchuk ta schan xuk'al banamile
li yanal te'etike chbajan
li sbek'take xch'ian
li abnaletike xnichimajik.

Ta yech'omal ave'e
ta jkejan jba ta banamil
chi nichimaj xchi'uk jk'elomtak.

GOTAS DEL DOLOR

Al rugido de tu voz
hombres y mujeres
derramaban gotas de dolor.

Con los ojos partidos
observan a la madre tierra
y reclaman su dolor.

¿Por qué?
¿por qué nos dicen indios?

Si en las cuatro estaciones del año
las hojas de los árboles caen
las semillas crecen
los campos florecen.

Al rugido de tu voz
me arrodillo a la tierra
y sigo floreciendo con mis retoños.

DROPS OF PAIN

The howling voices
of men and women
shed painful tears.

Wide-eyed, watching
Mother Earth
they weep.

Why?
Why do they call us "Indians"?

If the leaves fall
the seeds grow
the countryside flowers
and the land yields its bounty
throughout the four seasons?

Within their howling voice
I kneel on the earth
and flourish with my young shoots.

TA JK'AN JECHUN

Ta jk'an jechun k'ucha'al nichim ta abnaltik
Mu jk'an ts'unobal nichim
Ta jk'an jechun k'ucha'al mut nom ta xvil
Mu jk'an chukulun ta yech'omal ave'e.

Ta jk'an jechun k'ucha'al uk'um
ti mu'yuk xi'el ch anilaj ta sbe ach'ich'el
ta jk'an chi k'ejin chi tse'in ti buy ch'abal xi'ele.

Ta jk'an jechun k'ucha'al vo' ta vinajel
ti xbaj yalel ta abek'tale
ta jk'an jmuk'imtes li jk'ejimole
ta jujukoj yutsil vaichil.

QUIERO SER

Quiero ser una flor del campo
no la flor de tu jardín
quiero ser un ave que vuela
y no encadenada de tus palabras.

Quiero ser río
que corre sin miedo en tus venas
quiero cantar y sonreír sin miedo.

Quiera ser la lluvia
que cae sobre tu cuerpo
quiero elevar mi canto
al son de mis sueños.

I Want To Be

I want to be a flower in a field
not one in your garden
I want to be a bird that flies,
not chained by your words.

I want to be a river
running fearlessly through your veins
I want to sing and smile without fear.

I want to be the rain
that falls on your body
I want to raise my song
in the rhythm of my dreams.

Artemio Hernández

Iximetik

K'upil ti atalel
Ja' jechuk ti jtalel
Lekuk x'elan
Ma'uk skapobil sjol ats'unum.

Yox ti avanal
Umte, umte ti ach'iel
Ja' jechuk ti jkuxlej natijuk
Umte, umte ti jch'iel.

Mu me xa jel atalel
Mu me xjel jtalel
Te jechuk ti jkuxlej
Yox bajan xvinaj ti osile.

Mi xa laj ta taki ti'ile
K'opono yajval jo'
Mi xa laj ta k'ak'ale
K'opono yajval tok

Lekuk ti akuxlej
Lekuk ti jkuxlej
Mu atsatsalin aba
Mu jtsatsalin jba.

Milpas

Hermoso su forma de ser
Así sea mi forma de ser
Que perfecto
Que no molestan a tus hijos.

Tus hojas son verdes
Umté, umté tu nacer
Me das larga vida
Umté, umté mi vida.

No cambies de ser
No me cambies
Tal como soy, así seré
Así se verá el verde del paisaje.

Si te mueres sediento
Proclama al dueño de la lluvia
Si te mueres de calor
Proclama al dueño de las nubes.

Haz lo correcto
Hago lo correcto
No te niegues en ayudar
Me trasformo para ayudar

The Milpa

Your symmetry
Is my symmetry
Perfection
As your children grow.

Your green leaves,
Umté, umté your birth
You give me life
Umté, umté, my life.

Do not change
Don't change me
That I will be as I am
As the green countryside will be.

If you are dying of thirst,
Cry out to the Lord of the rain
If you are dying from the heat,
Cry out to the Lord of the clouds

Do what's right
I'll do what's right
If you need help, don't deny yourself
If you need help, I will change.

Tsajal Nichim

Amuil toj lek
Ja' jech toj t'ujomot
K'upil atalel
Unin tsajal nichim.

Xmuet amuil
Smuil atakupal
Tsajal nichim
Toj lek alekil

Ti atalele lek
Stalelal abektal
Stalelal achiel
Unin tsajal nichim

Xyometxa avanal
Tsajal nichim
Xmuet xa amuil
Umet xa jnichimal

Slamet xa ak'elel
Ja' ti lek ak'upijel
Lek avutsil
Ta atalel skupinoxuk.

Red Rose

Your scent seduces
You are so tender
You are perfect
Little red rose.

Your scent opens
The scent of your being
Red rose,
You are beauty itself.

You are amazing
You are exceptional
For being born
Little red rose.

Your leaves open
Red rose
Your essence diffuse
Your flower flowers

They observe your being
You are immanent
You are infinite
They love you for your being.

Xun Betan

PEPEN ANTS

Ak'otajan ants
ak'otajan
avole xk'eojin.

Ak'otajan ants
ak'otajan
kuxlejale smali xavil.

Ak'otajan ants
ak'otajan
ak'o nichimajuk jkuxlejale.

Ak'otajan ants
ak'otajan
yu'un ak'o jamuk
sna xch'ulel ko'ontontike.

Ch'ul vinajel xchi'uk osilaltike
smali xa jam axik'…

pepen.

MUJER MARIPOSA

Baila mujer
baila
tu hijo canta.

Baila mujer
baila
la vida espera tu vuelo.

Baila mujer
baila
haz florecer mi vida.

Baila mujer
baila
para abrir la casa
del espíritu de nuestro corazón.

El sagrado cielo y la tierra
esperan que extiendas tus alas…

mariposa.

BUTTERFLY WOMAN

Dance, woman,
dance
while your son sings.

Dance, woman,
dance
life is waiting for you to fly.

Dance, woman, dance
dance
you flower my life.

Dance woman,
dance
to open the house
 of our heart's spirit.

The sacred earth and sky
wait for you to extend your wings…
butterfly.

Oy Jvayojelkotik Ta Kuxlejal

Bak'in li ayane, mu jna' bu li liktal
ta xambal ta chobtik la kojtikin jba
li k'ot ta sk'ob jmuk'tatotak
lekil ch'ul balumil la snak'ben jmixik'.

Ch'ul ja'mal la jxan, la jk'ejinta ch'ul ik'
la jambe sti' ch'ul tok, la jambe sti' osilaltik
la kuch'be ya'lel ch'ul uk'um, ya'lel sat vo'
ch'ul nichim, ch'ul ixim la jts'un ta jvun.

Ta ch'ul vits li ak'otaj, la jlok'ta ch'ul k'anal
la jk'oponta jlumal, la sts'ibabe xchopolal
li avan ta stojol chopolal, la jta vokolil
la jmey jchi'iltak, la jtsak te jluke.

Mu jna' bu li liktal
ja' to bak'in la smilik jchi'iltake
mu jna' bu li liktal
ja' to bak'in la spojik jlumalkotike
mu jna' bu li liktal
ja' no'ox la jchanbe jm'e jtot yavanel la'banel,
la jchanbeik sa'el kolel,
lekilal xchi'uk ich'el ta muk'.
la jchan yalel:

xkil jbatik ono'ox ta sbatel osil…!

Somos Jóvenes Con Sueños

Cuando nací, no sabía quien era
caminando en la milpa me encontré
llegué a los brazos de mis abuelos
hermosa tierra que guarda mi ombligo.

Caminé las montañas y canté al viento
abrí las puertas de las nubes y del tiempo
bebí agua de los ríos y de arroyos
sembré flores y maíz en mis libros.

Bailé en las montañas y dibujé las estrellas
leí los pueblos y escribí las injusticias
grité a los corruptos y enfrenté el dolor
abracé a mis hermanos y agarré el azadón.

No sabía quien soy
hasta que mataron a mis hermanos.
No sabía quien soy
hasta que nos quitaron nuestras tierras.
No sabía quien soy,
pero aprendí de mis abuelos a denunciar la tiranía, a luchar
por la libertad,
la justicia y la dignidad.
Aprendí a decir:

¡hasta la victoria siempre…!

The Young Dreamers

When I was born I didn't know who I was
walking through the milpa I found myself
in the arms of my grandparents
the beautiful earth where my umbilical cord is buried.

I walked in the mountains and sang to the wind
I opened the doors of the clouds, the doors of time
I drank water from the rivers and streams
I planted flowers and corn in my books.

I danced in the mountains and drew the stars
I read people and recorded injustice
I denounced corruption and confronted pain
I embraced my brothers and grabbed the hoe.

I didn't know who I was
until they killed my brothers
I didn't know who I was
until they took our land.
I didn't know who I was
but I learned from my ancestors to denounce tyranny, to
    fight for liberty,
for justice, for dignity.
I learned to say:

  ¡hasta la victoria siempre...!

jVayuchiletik/The Dreamers

Artemio Hernández: was born in Ts'uts'ben, San Andrés Larrainzar. He currently studies Human Development. He is a singer/songwriter, and has participated in numerous poetry recitals. He holds the position of substitute community agente in his home town.

Candelaria Álvarez is from Bochilte', Huixtan, Chiapas. She is currently a student in the Department of Language and Culture, and has taken several classes on writing and epigraphy. She has published previously as a member of Sichimal Vayuchil and in the literary magazine *Conmoción*.

Cecilia Díaz is a writer and poet from San Andrés Larrainzar, Chiapas. She has participated in colloquia and conferences in indigenous education and cosmovision. In addition her work as a poet and translator has appeared in *Snichimal Vayuchil*, *Conmoción*, y *Sbek' Vun*.

Manu Pukuj is from Yibel Osil, Chenalhó, Chiapas. He has been doing research on the milpa as organized by the Tsotsil agricultural calendar. He presently coordinates ecological projects in rural communities and organizes events on Maya spiritual and cultural development.

Paty López was born in the community of Yutniotic in the municipio of San Juan Chamula, Chiapas. She is a student in the Department of Languahe and Culture. She has taken part in a number of workshops on creative writing and youth leadership.

Ruve K'ulej is from Chilil, Huixtan, Chiapas. He has a BA in Sustainable Development. During his academic career he participated in a number of different seminars and workshops on agroecology, the environment, and sustainability. His work has appeared previously in literary magazines and collective anthologies.

Susi Bentzulul is from San Juan Chamula. She holds a degree in Language and Culture, and has participated in workshops in youth leadership and creative writing. She has published her work in collective anthologies and online, in venues such as *Snichimal Vayuchil* and the magazine *Conmoción*.

Tino Sántiz is originally from Aldama, Chiapas, and he is currently as student in Language and Culture. He has worked in educational leadership. He has been a participant in painting and literary workshops, and has published his work in a number of literary magazines and collective anthologies.

Xun Betan was born in Venustiano Carranza, Chiapas. He is the coordinator of the **Snichimal Vayuchil: experiment in bats'i k'op** project, as well as **Sna Jk'optik Press**. He has translated and published a number of books. In addition, he is part of the **Espejo Somos** collective, and on the board of *Conmoción*.

About the Authors

Paul Worley is Associate Professor of Global Literature at Western Carolina University, and Editor-at-Large for Mexico at the journal of world literature in translation, *Asymptote*. He has forthcoming translations of the award winning indigenous poets Hubert Malina (Mé'pháá) and Martín Tonalmeyotl (Nahuátl). He published *Telling and Being Told: Storytelling and Cultural Control in Contemporary Yucatec Maya*, and, in 2013, has recently published articles in *A contracorriente*, *Studies in American Indian Literatures*, and *Latin American Caribbean Ethnic Studies*. Stories recorded as part of his research on Maya literatures are available at tsikbalichmaya.org.

Gloria E. Chacón is Assistant Professor in the Literature department at UCSD. She received her Ph.D. in Literature from the University of California Santa Cruz. Postdoctoral work in the Native American Studies Department at the University of California Davis and a CLIR Fellowship at UCLA's Charles Young Research Library has shaped her interdisciplinary and transnational approach to indigenous literatures. Chacón's work has appeared in *Cuadernos de Literatura* (Colombia), in *Diversidad y diálogo intercultural a través de las literaturas en lenguas mexicanas* (Mexico), *Poéticas y Políticas* (Germany), *Revista de Estudios Latinoamericanos* (Canada), and *Latino Studies* (USA). She has also co-edited (with Juan Sánchez) a special issue focused on indigenous literature for *Diálogo* (USA) and is currently working on a co-edited anthology, *Indigenous Interfaces*, with Jennifer Gómez. Her book, *Indigenous Cosmolectics: Kab'awil and the Making of Maya and Zapotec Literatures* is under contract with UNC Press (forthcoming 2018).

www.ingramcontent.com/pod-product-compliance
Lightning Source LLC
Chambersburg PA
CBHW070457050426
42449CB00012B/3012